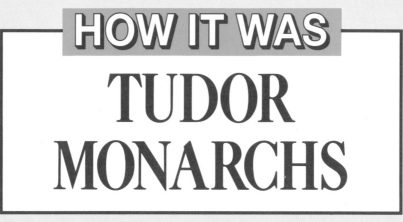

HOW IT WAS
TUDOR MONARCHS

Jessica Saraga

B T Batsford Ltd, London

CONTENTS

942·05

7090
1

Photoset by Deltatype Ltd, Ellesmere Port, Cheshire and printed in Hong Kong

Published by B. T. Batsford Ltd
4 Fitzhardinge Street, London W1H 0AH

A CIP catalogue record for this book is available from the British Library

ISBN 0 7134 6350 3

Frontispiece: A miniature of Elizabeth I.
Cover: The Field of the Cloth of Gold.

2

INTRODUCTION

The sixteenth century was the century of the Tudors. The first Tudor monarch, Henry VII, came to the throne 15 years before the start of the sixteenth century, and the last Tudor monarch, Queen Elizabeth I, died just three years after its end.

The Tudor period is a well-known one. Most people have heard of King Henry VIII and his six wives. They have heard of Mary I, whom they may know as 'Bloody Mary', and of Mary Queen of Scots, her cousin. Almost everyone in this country has heard of Queen Elizabeth I, and the popular stories of her reign. They know that Sir Walter Raleigh is supposed to have laid down his cloak in the mud for the Queen to walk on, so that she should not dirty her shoes, and that Sir Francis Drake is supposed to have insisted on finishing his game of bowls on Plymouth Hoe before setting out to fight the Spanish Armada.

People remember the Tudor period, too, for its houses, with their distinctive black timbers and white plaster, and for its literature. The reign of Queen Elizabeth is often remembered as the age of Shakespeare (though, in fact, just as much of Shakespeare's writing life fell in the reign of her successor, James I, as in Elizabeth's reign).

Surprisingly, we owe many of our ideas about the Tudors to the writers and painters of the nineteenth century, who particularly admired the Elizabethan age, and used it as the subject of their poetry and plays. One thing which caught their imagination was the fighting at sea between English and Spanish seamen. They tended to write dramatically about the patriotism and heroism of the English seamen. Alfred, Lord Tennyson, for example, wrote about Sir Richard Grenville, and his ship, the *Revenge*, captured by the Spanish after a heroic stand.

> 'I have fought for Queen and Faith like a valiant man and true;
> I have only done my duty as a man is bound to do:
> With a joyful spirit I Sir Richard Grenville die!'
> And he fell upon their decks and he died.

Sir Henry Newbolt wrote about Drake in similar vein, using a mock Devon speech to imitate Drake's own:

> Drake he's in his hammock till the great Armada's come,
> (Capten, art tha sleepin' there below?),
> Slung atween the round shot, listenin' for the drum,
> An' dreamin' arl the time o' Plymouth Hoe.

The way these poets and painters presented the Tudor period may reveal more about their own Victorian values than about the Tudor age itself. Victorians valued courage, duty, patriotism, and the idea that Britain was more powerful than other countries. What did Tudors themselves value? What did they think about their kings and queens? What we really need to look at to illuminate the history of the Tudor period is its own writings and art. This is what you can begin to do in this book.

Introductory Quiz

Do you know
how the Wars of the Roses ended?

who built Hampton Court?

the names of Henry VIII's three children?

who Lady Jane Grey was?

what the Spanish Armada was?

what propaganda means?

RULERS AND SUBJECTS

When people learn about the history of twentieth-century Britain a few hundred years from now, kings and queens will not be a major topic. Yet in the history of the sixteenth century in England, kings and queens – and not just the monarchs themselves, but their husbands and wives too – figure very prominently. Can you think why this should be so?

The most important reason is that history tends to be written about people who are powerful, and in the sixteenth century power was wielded by monarchs. This means that the monarch made all the important decisions about how to run the country – whether the country should go to war with another country, what form of religion the people of the country should have, who they could trade with, and who should be responsible for law and order in the localities, and administer justice.

What is more, the monarchs were very rich. They had enough income of their own to live in great style and luxury in comparison with their subjects. When they needed more money for a war or emergency, they had the power to tax their subjects to pay for it.

Of course, monarchs had their advisers (called the council), usually drawn from the richer of their subjects, the aristocracy. Cardinal Wolsey, who advised Henry VIII, was an exception, since he was the son of a butcher (some historians say an innkeeper). He was able to become powerful because he was exceptionally clever, and managed to get an education through the church, becoming a priest, then a bishop and eventually Archbishop of York and a Cardinal (one of the top officials of the Catholic church).

But it was almost unheard of for a poor boy to become as rich or as powerful as Wolsey did. Most people died in the same economic conditions as those in which they were born. They would never even entertain any hopes of becoming any richer than they were; they would concentrate on trying to avoid starvation, and praying that the harvest would not fail. These are the people we do not hear about in history. They lived and suffered and loved and laughed and left no records. We can try to piece together ideas about their lives from shreds of evidence in pictures, such as this one showing men and women harvesting in the fields. We can find out the bare details about their baptisms, marriages and funerals in parish records, but we can never hope to know as much about them as we do about their rulers whose decisions affected their lives.

Women in particular have been missed out of history. The picture showing women at work as well as men is an unusual one. Women in most eras of history had to obey first their fathers, and then, when they married, their husbands. It was very rare in the sixteenth century for a woman to be able to record her thoughts or feelings, because women rarely knew how to write.

It is therefore rather surprising to note that two of the five Tudor monarchs were women. Between them, Mary and Elizabeth reigned for nearly half of the 118 years of the Tudor period. When Mary came to the throne in 1553, she had to assert her right over another female claimant, Lady Jane Grey. Elizabeth, too, had a female rival to the throne in Mary Queen of Scots. The reason for this is that *legitimacy* (being the true child of your parents) was considered very important. Men would accept a female monarch with a proven right to the throne more readily than a male monarch without one.

Sometimes people deny that women have been left out of history, and that women were powerless in society, pointing to these queens as examples. But they are forgetting what isolated examples they were. In general, women were considered to be nothing more than the property of men. It is particularly interesting, therefore, to see how these queens managed to assert their power over men, and how men responded to it.

We must not forget that we are being very selective indeed in studying these five monarchs. The millions of their subjects who have left not even a footprint in history are nonetheless just as much a part of the past. When you have read this book, you should consider whether you would like to learn about these ordinary people, as well as their monarchs.

This painting of peasants bringing in the harvest is one of the few pictures we have of ordinary people in the Tudor period. This painting is from a Flemish Book of Hours.

People power

Although ordinary people were at the mercy of their monarchs and the aristocracy, they had ways of making their presence felt. This is an anonymous verse which was nailed on to the door of a Coventry church in the reign of Henry VII, warning of the anger of ordinary people.

> Litell small been
> That all about fleen
>   They waggen their whyng.
> Where as they light,
> The been will byte,
>   And also styng.
> Loke that ye do right.
> Both day and night,
>   Beware of wappys.

(Quoted in *English Historical Review*, ix, 1984)

Unequal pay

This is part of a regulation fixing maximum wages.

A man servant of the best sort shall not have more by the year than, with a livery [uniform], xls.
The best sort of women servants shall not have more by the year than with a livery, xxis.

(Hertford Session Rolls, 1591–2)

If 'xls' means 40 shillings, can you work out how much 'xxis' is, and what proportion, roughly, of a man's wage might be paid to a woman?'

From the text and illustrations in this chapter what can we learn about how hard Tudor women worked?

'Fleen' means 'fly'; 'light' means 'land'. What do you think 'been' and 'wappys' are?

Who are the 'been' and 'wappys' here?

What will they do? Do you think the richer members of society had much to fear from them?

CAN YOU WORK OUT ?

why kings and queens are less important in history now than they were in Tudor times?

CHECK YOUR UNDERSTANDING

What do the following words mean?
Cardinal
Legitimacy

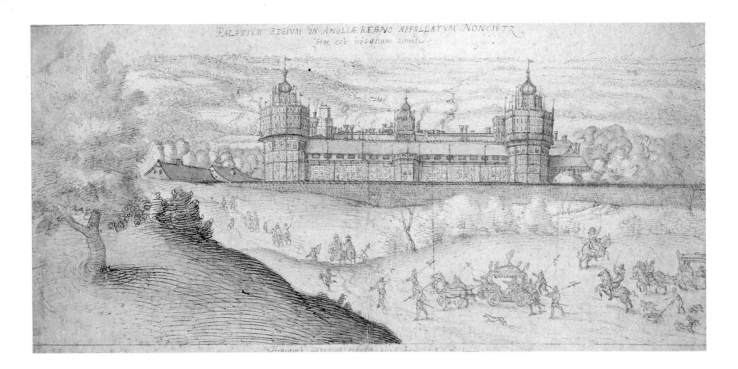

This picture shows the kind of scale on which monarchs were able to build. Nonsuch Palace was built in the 1530s and '40s for King Henry VIII. It was Queen Elizabeth's favourite royal residence.

Ordinary people's houses have almost all disappeared, because they could not afford to use durable building materials. They would have been functional rather than decorated like Nonsuch.

CAN YOU REMEMBER ?

what kind of powers Tudor monarchs had over their subjects' lives?

THINGS TO DO

1   Find out about a Tudor house in your area. Discover who built it and owned it. How wealthy was the family? Were they landowners? If you can visit the house, make a list of the status symbols (such as family portraits, and expensive, imported goods) that are still there.

2   Find some reproductions of portraits of Tudor monarchs. Compare them with photographs and cartoons of prominent people which you find in newspapers today. Are there any similarities?

Historians have traditionally thought of the Tudor dynasty as the first dynasty (family of rulers) of what they call the 'modern' period, following on from the medieval period, or Middle Ages. History books lump the Tudors together because they fit – or nearly fit – conveniently into the sixteenth century. However, the Tudor period was a century of very noticeable changes, and so Henry VII and his subjects at the end of the fifteenth century probably had much more in common with the people of Edward IV's reign in the 1470s than they did with Henry's granddaughter Elizabeth I and her subjects a century later.

The changes of the late fifteenth and sixteenth centuries were economic, social and religious. Most people still lived, as they had for centuries, by growing their own food on a plot of land, which they would probably rent from a lord or gentleman, though some people would own their own. The rigid feudal relationships of the Middle Ages, in which landlords would guarantee land and protection to their tenants and the tenants would have to work and fight for their lord in return, had disappeared. Indeed, some landlords, far from holding their tenants to their feudal obligations and preventing them from moving away, as medieval landlords had done, were pulling down their houses and driving their tenants away. This was because they now wanted to use the land for sheep farming instead of renting it out to tenants; wool could be sold for increasingly high prices. The fences put round the land to keep the sheep in gave the name *enclosure* to this changeover to raising sheep. Driving tenants off the land was called *depopulation*.

Victims of depopulation would inevitably become *vagrants* (homeless beggars) for a while. They would be unlikely to find work as agricultural wage labourers, because widespread enclosure was putting many others into the same situation. It was also decreasing the amount of agricultural work available – it took fewer workers to look after sheep. At the same time, the population was growing, so more people than before would be competing for work.

But, if they were lucky, unemployed people might find work in the towns, which were growing rapidly in the Tudor period. They would not be able to break into the prosperous world of crafts and trade, but townspeople might employ them for menial work, for towns were generally thriving. This was a world of buying and selling, of earning money to buy food and clothes rather than growing and making everything you needed. It was a world inhabited by growing numbers of Tudor people – sailors (for many towns were ports), boatmen (to provide transport), apprentices, shopkeepers, innkeepers, *ostlers*, saddlers, and the host of servants of prosperous people. In London, as the monarchs increasingly spent more time there, there were large numbers of servants of the royal court. In the picture, you can see some of the better-off Tudor people, with some of their children and pets, at a wedding in Bermondsey, just south of the Thames in London. There are servants, too, and in the background on the river, some of the large numbers of people who made their living on the Thames. Across the Thames is the Tower of London.

Another feature of the Tudor period was *inflation*. High food prices, and wages that did not keep up with them, added to the problems of the unemployed. Historians disagree about the reason why prices rose so drastically, but the most likely one is simply that the supply of food could not be increased to meet the needs of the expanding population. High prices therefore added to the problems caused by enclosure and depopulation. The problems were made even worse when Henry VIII closed down the monasteries and nunneries in the 1530s, since these establishments had always looked after the poor.

This *dissolution* (or closing) of the monasteries was part of another vital change of the Tudor period, the Reformation. The Reformation changed the status of the church in England. It was no longer part of the Catholic church controlled by the Pope, as it had been in Henry VII's reign, and Henry VIII's until the 1530s. It was now a separate Church of England with the monarch as its head. It became a Protestant church, which meant that its members objected to all kinds of practices which they associated with Catholicism, from the use of incense and candles in church, to the idea of praying to the saints or the Virgin Mary rather than to God. How the Reformation came about is described in later chapters.

A wedding in Bermondsey, just south of London.

Enclosures

Sir Thomas More, who was a famous scholar and statesman of Henry VIII's reign, was very concerned about the effects of enclosure and depopulation. In his book about an imaginary ideal country, *Utopia*, he described what was happening in England, like this:

> Hundreds of farmers are evicted and . . . out the poor creatures have to go – men and women, husbands and wives, widows and orphans, mothers and tiny children. Out they have to go from the homes that they know so well, and they can't find anywhere else to live. What can they do but steal – and be very properly hanged? Of course they can always become tramps and beggars, but even then they're liable to be arrested as vagrants, and put in prison for being idle, when nobody will give them a job, however much they want one. For farm work is what they're used to, and where there's no arable land, there's no farm work to be had.

(Sir Thomas More, *Utopia*)

In the sixteenth century the only solution seemed to be to make enclosures illegal, but it was hard to enforce this. Landlords were prepared to break the law because they were making so much money out of enclosures. There were also laws which said that a vagrant (provided he was able-bodied and capable of work) could be

> tied to the end of a cart naked and be beaten with whips throughout the same market town or other place till his body be bloody by reason of such whipping and after such punishment . . . the person so punished . . . shall . . . return forthwith without delay . . . straightway to the place where he was born . . . and there put himself to labour.

(Beggars Act, 1531)

It was only at the end of the reign of Elizabeth I that people began to stop blaming beggars for being destitute, and to realize that most vagrants begged from necessity, not because they wanted to. Do you think people get blamed for being poor today?

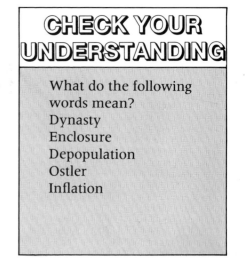

Q

Do you think the problem of homelessness is as severe today as it was when Sir Thomas More described it?

Do you still see vagrants or beggars today?

CAN YOU WORK OUT ?

Food prices rose in the sixteenth century because the rising population meant there was not enough food to go round. Can you work out why enclosure made food prices go up even faster?

CHECK YOUR UNDERSTANDING

What do the following words mean?
Dynasty
Enclosure
Depopulation
Ostler
Inflation

In this woodcut, a vagrant is being punished by being dragged around the town and whipped. In the background, a criminal is being hanged.

THINGS TO DO

1 See if you can make out the boats and boatmen on the River Thames in the picture of Bermondsey on page 9. The guests at the wedding might well have come across the river by boat. Make a list of the methods of transport you yourself use. Does it include water transport? If it does not, say why you prefer other methods.

2 In a group of four or five, imagine you are Tudor Justices of the Peace, in charge of local law and order, and discuss what can be done about the problems of vagrants, who come into your area and beg or steal. Is it their fault? Is there any work for them to do? Is it your duty to feed them if they are hungry?

Henry Tudor had a weak claim to the throne; he seized it purely out of ambition. But, though none of his four predecessors on the throne had managed to hold on to it securely, Henry became a successful king, reigning for 24 years until his death in 1509.

So Henry VII's accession marked a kind of turning point. The civil wars known as the Wars of the Roses came to an end, and political stability was established. The five Tudor monarchs reigned between them for a total of 118 years, successfully resisting any challenge to their right to rule. So, despite being founded on a doubtful claim, the Tudor dynasty survived, only dying out with Elizabeth I, who had no children.

Elizabeth of York, Henry VII's wife, by an unknown artist.

This was achieved partly because Henry VII united the two houses of Lancaster and York, who had fought the Wars of the Roses. He himself was the Lancastrian candidate for the throne. He defeated the Yorkist King Richard III in battle in 1485; he then married Richard's niece, the Yorkist Princess Elizabeth. So their children were of the houses of both Lancaster and York, and they wore the new Tudor rose, both red and white, as a badge of this union.

It was not all easy, though; Henry VII was still threatened by other Yorkist claimants to the throne, and by two *impostors*, Lambert Simnel and Perkin Warbeck, put forward by Yorkist supporters. But Henry's intelligence service was good. He was warned of these plots, and of which of his courtiers had wavering loyalties, so he was able to act in good time. He was also quite prepared to execute anyone who could be a threat. He put to death the last Yorkist with a serious claim to the throne, the Earl of Warwick, in 1499. The Earl of Warwick was a young man of 24 who had been held in the Tower of London ever since Henry VII first seized the throne in 1485, when Warwick was ten. He was hardly a great danger, but he was convicted of plotting with Perkin Warbeck. Perhaps he really had been involved in a conspiracy; perhaps he was framed by the king's agents. In any case, no doubt the king rested easier once he was finally out of the way.

This portrait of Henry VII was painted in 1505. How can we match the person we see in the painting to what we know about Henry's life? His face is set, his jaw is determined; he seems to be smiling but we will never know why. He looks like a fair man and, indeed, he did treat most of his subjects fairly (though not the Earl of Warwick). His face seems to reflect the kindness he showed to his family (though he did not treat the family of his wife, the Yorkists, kindly). Most of all the painting seems to show Henry's wariness: he knew that he had won the throne by invasion and battle and that, unless he was constantly prepared, somebody else could do the same to him.

During his reign, Henry commissioned a chapel to be built in Westminster Abbey. He intended it to be a *shrine* (a holy place) dedicated to Henry VI. Henry VI was the last Lancastrian king to reign

Henry VII, by Michael Sittow, 1505.

before the Yorkists took over in 1461. Henry Tudor hoped to have Henry VI declared a saint by the Pope. This would encourage the idea that the Lancastrians, including himself, were therefore the rightful royal line enjoying God's blessing. But this *propaganda* (political advertising giving only one point of view) scheme was never completed, though the chapel itself eventually was, after Henry VII's death. Once the next king, Henry VIII, had succeeded his father peacefully, the Tudor line was established, and there was less need for propaganda, though, as we shall see in later chapters, it was always a feature of Tudor rule.

When he died, Henry VII left England a wealthy, orderly and, on the whole, law-abiding country. He encouraged trade, particularly the export of wool, which was England's main product, and he avoided war because it would have been too expensive. He won the support of the land-owning gentry who, as Justices of the Peace, were prepared to take charge of local law and order voluntarily, without pay. This was because, as property owners, they would have had the most to lose if law enforcement had broken down.

Henry was not the most popular of kings. He was aloof and stern, always insisting on the respect due to his position. But he left England at peace, and better off financially than any of the rest of his dynasty were to do.

You read in Rulers and Subjects about how women in history are often ignored. Little is known about Henry VII's Queen, though she and Henry are thought to have had a loving relationship. She had eight children, of whom only three lived to be adults. Here are some of the things that history doesn't tell us about her:

—whether she considered running away when Henry Tudor killed her uncle, Richard III, at the Battle of Bosworth.
—her reaction when she was told she was to marry Henry.
—her feelings when her husband executed her cousin, the Earl of Warwick.
—her feelings when five of her children died.

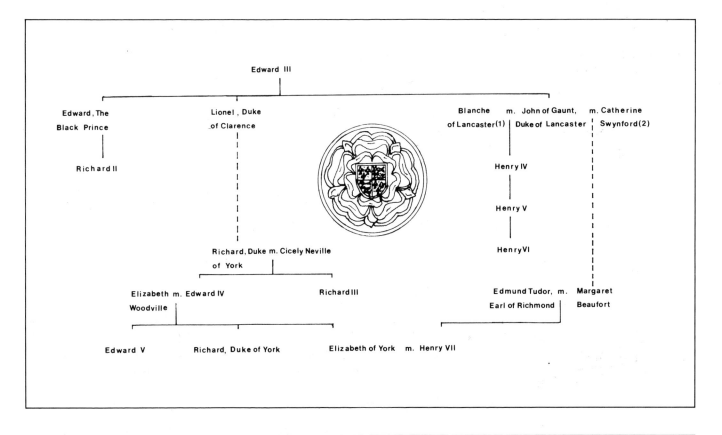

This family tree shows the union of the houses of York and Lancaster, and the beginning of the Tudor dynasty.

THINGS TO DO

1 Copy out the family tree, and draw a white rose on the Yorkist side, and a red rose on the Lancastrian side. You could design a *portcullis* emblem, too; this was used by earlier English monarchs, and taken over by the Tudors.

2 Decide whether you would have been a loyal subject of Henry VII if you had been alive during his reign. Draw a diagram or cartoon of Henry, emphasizing either his good or bad qualities. Have a good look at the illustration on page 13 before you start, and remember that in cartoons words can be just as important as the sketch or diagram itself.

Henry VII and the economy

Here are two views of Henry VII:

> Being a King that loved wealth and treasure, he could not endure to have trade sick.
>
> (Sir Francis Bacon, *History of King Henry VII*).

> Above all else he cherished justice: and consequently he punished with the utmost vigour, robberies, murder, and every other kind of crime. But in his later days all these virtues were obscured by avarice . . . In a monarch it is . . . the worst form of all vices, since it hurts everyone.
>
> (Polydore Vergil, *English History*)

Avarice means greed. Both these writers suggest that Henry VII loved money. Do you think he desired personal wealth, mainly, or wealth for England?

Polydore Vergil was an Italian who came to England in 1502. He wrote his history about 100 years before Bacon wrote his. Is this a reason to accept what he says more readily than what Bacon says?

Does it make any difference that Henry VII himself asked Vergil to write his history? Do *you* believe what Bacon and Vergil say about him?

Which of the following descriptions do you think fit Henry VII:

a man with a good grasp of economics and politics

a warm-hearted extrovert

a man with a keen sense of family

a ruthless and ambitious man

a man who became wiser as he got older?

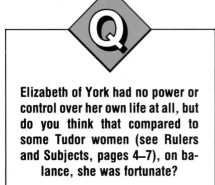

Elizabeth of York had no power or control over her own life at all, but do you think that compared to some Tudor women (see Rulers and Subjects, pages 4–7), on balance, she was fortunate?

CHECK YOUR UNDERSTANDING

What do the following words mean?

Impostor
Shrine
Propaganda

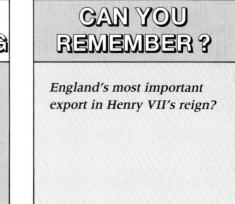

CAN YOU REMEMBER ?

England's most important export in Henry VII's reign?

When Henry VII died in 1509, the new Tudor king was his 17-year-old second son, Henry. His elder son, Arthur, had died in 1501, soon after marrying Catherine, the daughter of the King of Aragon and the Queen of Castile. (Aragon and Castile were two separate parts of what is now Spain.) By getting married, Ferdinand of Aragon and Isabella of Castile made Spain into one country.

Henry VIII inherited not just the throne which had been destined for his brother Arthur, but also Arthur's widow. Henry and Catherine made a striking couple. She was an attractive young woman of 22, with grey eyes and long, golden-brown hair. When she rode in procession through London with Henry on the eve of their coronation, she wore her hair loose down her back. Her young husband, though five years her junior, was already tall and athletic, auburn-haired and clear-complexioned. It is a pity that we have no well-known portraits which successfully portray Henry's good looks before they began to decay. It is as the overweight victim of disease and excess that we tend to think of him.

For Henry liked to live life, as we might say today, in the fast lane. Perhaps this was because his father had never allowed him any freedom or responsibility, which as a teenager Henry found annoying. Once he was his own master – in fact the whole country's master – he threw himself into continuous activity and pleasure, clearly revelling in doing just as he liked. In 1511 his activities were described as shooting, singing, dancing, wrestling, casting of the bar, playing the recorder, flute and virginals, setting of songs, making of ballads, hunting and hawking. He also gambled, ate and drank without restraint.

He was rash in public policy, too. Inexperienced, immature and impressed by romantic notions of knights and chivalry, he was determined to win glory on the battlefield. He was also determined to win the throne of France, to which English kings traditionally laid claim. He knew men whose grandfathers had fought at the Battle of Agincourt (an English victory over the French in 1415). He wanted to match the success of Henry V, who had led the English army at Agincourt. Against the advice of some of the more cautious members of his council, Henry prepared for war.

He was at war for much of his reign, not always with France and not often successfully. He won no glorious victories, and the nearest he came to imitating the practices of chivalry was at a meeting with the French King Francis I in peacetime in 1520. Huge amounts of money were spent by both monarchs in impressing the other. The meeting took place at Guisnes, just outside Calais, which was a small area of English territory in France. Queen Catherine and the royal court were shipped over to Calais, preceded by vast quantities of food and finery, such magnificence that the site at Guisnes became known as the Field of the Cloth of Gold. You can see from the illustration on the cover how splendid the scene must have been. You can see the houses and castle at Guisnes, the tents for accommodation, and the spectacular summer palace erected for the occasion. On the back cover is the king on his horse.

Behind this whole operation was the organizing genius of Cardinal Wolsey (see page 19). From about 1513 Wolsey had been climbing to prominence in the state, gaining increasing influence over the young king by doing the more boring tasks of government and administration for him. He had successfully taken charge of the organization of war supplies, and now, under his direction, the expedition to Calais went like clockwork.

By 1520 Wolsey had become Lord Chancellor of England, which meant that he was at the head of the country's legal administration and presided over the House of Lords when Parliament met. He was a Papal Legate (a representative of the Pope), which gave him power over all aspects of the church in England too. He had begun to build a huge palace for himself by the Thames at Hampton Court and was becoming, some people said, even grander than the king. His palace had 1000 rooms, and he had a staff of 500 to run it. From his income, which he received from his bishoprics and abbeys, he was as rich as the king.

Hampton Court Palace was the palace Cardinal Wolsey had built for himself.

Henry VIII in love (1)

Here is a poem Henry VIII wrote to Catherine of Aragon:

> As the holly groweth green,
> and never changeth hue
> so I am, ever hath been,
> unto my lady true.
>
> (Printed in Stevens, *Music and poetry in the Early Tudor Court*)

One of Henry VIII's favourite pastimes was jousting. Here, he is jousting in a tournament watched by Catherine of Aragon, his first wife.

The Battle of Flodden

Despite Henry VIII's desire for victory and glory in France, the most decisive military victory achieved in his reign was over the Scots. It was the Battle of Flodden, won by the Earl of Surrey in 1513. Henry himself was not even there, being away fighting in France at the time. But it was a disaster for the Scots. Their king, James IV, was killed, and with him many of the Scottish nobility. Here is part of a ballad about it.

> To tell you plain, twelve thousand were slain
> That to the fight did stand
> And many prisoners took that day
> The best in all Scotland.
>
> That day made many a fatherless child
> And many a widow poor
> And many a Scottish gay lady
> Sat weeping in her bower.

The latest theory about Henry VIII's health is that, amazingly, he was suffering from malnutrition. The sixteenth-century idea of a healthy diet was to eat as much meat as possible, and to drink ale or wine. Food was affected by snobbery. Milk, cheese, eggs and vegetables were thought to be fit only for peasants; fruit was thought to give you bad skin and 'putrified fevers' (Sir Thomas Elyot, *Castel of Helth*, 1539). On a diet like this, Henry VIII was suffering from severe vitamin deficiency and, in particular, the scurvy which results from insufficient vitamin C. Scurvy patients suffer from leg ulcers, rashes, loose teeth and swollen gums, lethargy, moodiness, constipation, bad breath and a bloated body, all of which symptoms were noticed in Henry VIII in his later years.

Cardinal Wolsey

Cardinal Wolsey came from low origins (see Rulers and Subjects, pages 4–7). Once in the church, he rose to the top by being clever and efficient. But he was resented by the aristocracy and gentry, who felt it was their exclusive right to exercise power, and to influence the king. Snobbery has always been a feature of English society, and the Tudor period was no exception. This description of Wolsey illustrates the kind of behaviour which annoyed people.

> This Cardinal is the person who rules both the King and the entire kingdom. On the ambassador's first arrival in England Wolsey used to say to him, 'His Majesty will do (whatever it was)': then, gradually, he went forgetting himself, and started saying, '*We* shall do it': now he has reached the point where he is saying, 'I shall do it'.
>
> (Giustiniani, *Despatches to the Venetian Court*)

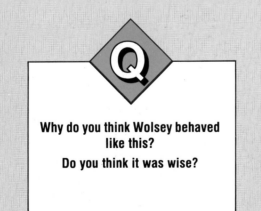

Q

Why do you think Wolsey behaved like this?
Do you think it was wise?

THINGS TO DO

1   Draw up a diet sheet for Henry VIII, which would have enabled him to regain his health. You will need to check which foods were available in sixteenth-century England.

2   Using the information in this chapter and the chapter on Henry VII, make a list of differences in character and appearance between father and son.

3   Find some more pictures of Tudor aristocratic costume, and make a collage to illustrate it. You could use scraps of fabric, or cut-up colour magazines and wrapping paper. Paper doilies make good ruffs.

4   Make a group or class collage of the Field of the Cloth of Gold.

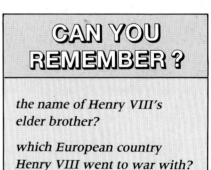

CAN YOU REMEMBER ?

the name of Henry VIII's elder brother?

which European country Henry VIII went to war with?

what a Papal Legate was?

By 1525 Henry VIII was 34, experienced, if not very successful, in battle and an experienced ruler, though he relied heavily on Cardinal Wolsey, whose appetite for hard work never seemed to diminish. Older, wiser, his body now showing signs of abuse and disease, perhaps Henry began to be conscious that he was not immortal. But to safeguard the Tudor dynasty, which was still only 40 years old, it was of vital importance to have a male heir, in case there was armed rebellion at his death. Henry had no male heir. He and Catherine had had a baby boy in 1511, but the child had only lived for seven weeks. Three more boys were born in the next few years, but the only child who survived was a girl, Mary, born in 1516. By 1525 Catherine was nearly 40, and now unlikely to have any more children.

Henry began to wonder if the lack of a male heir was a punishment from God, because he had married his brother's widow, which was against church law. He had, before he married her, received permission from the Pope for the marriage, but he began to think that perhaps God's laws could not be so easily bypassed. Catherine herself insisted that she and Prince Arthur had never consummated their marriage, and so she had still been a virgin when she married Henry. In this case, there would be no question of their having broken a religious law anyway. But Henry would not support her version of what had happened. He was beginning to think in terms of divorce, and remarriage. By 1528 he was falling in love with a young lady of the court, Anne Boleyn. It made him even more determined.

Although the 'king's great matter', as people at the time called it, is usually referred to as a divorce, what Henry wanted was an *annulment* (a declaration that his marriage was not, and had never been, legally valid). This would free him to marry Anne Boleyn. It was the Pope who would have to make this declaration, and in 1527 Henry told Wolsey to arrange it.

There were three problems. First of all, Wolsey, despite his high rank in the church, did not have much influence with Pope Clement VII. Secondly, Pope Clement was much more in awe of the Holy Roman Emperor, whose armies were conquering Italy, and from whose captivity Clement had only just managed to escape. And this Holy Roman Emperor, whom Clement was anxious to avoid offending, was none other than Charles, King of Spain, the son of Catherine's elder sister Juana. The Emperor was very unlikely to allow the Pope to go along with such an insult to Catherine of Aragon, his own aunt. The third problem was that the Pope did not believe in the justice of Henry's case anyway; he believed the marriage was perfectly valid.

Despite this, he did eventually send a representative, Cardinal Campeggio, who heard the case at Blackfriars in 1529, but after six months the court adjourned without making a decision. It looked as if Henry had failed. Henry blamed Wolsey, stripped him of the Lord Chancellorship and took Hampton Court from him. The king was no longer the golden boy of 1509; he was selfish, heartless and ruthless, and was becoming the massive, heavy-jowled figure familiar to us from paintings.

This portrait of Henry VIII was painted in 1541, six years before his death.

This painting of Henry VIII with his three children and Jane Seymour is now at Hampton Court.

He was a man who demanded his own way, and in the matter of the divorce, he got it. The consequences of Henry getting his divorce are still with us. Because the Pope would not allow the divorce, Henry removed the whole of the English church from the Pope's control. With the advice of a new and able minister, Thomas Cromwell, he bullied the clergy into accepting this move and appointed a new Archbishop of Canterbury, Thomas Cranmer, who would grant him the divorce. By 1533 he had both a new wife, Anne Boleyn, and a new heir. The heir was a girl, the future Queen Elizabeth I.

It was not until 1536 that Henry finally managed to produce a male heir. He had executed Anne Boleyn for alleged adultery, and then married her cousin Jane Seymour, who was the baby Prince Edward's mother. Only 12 days after giving birth, she died.

He married three more times after this, Anne of Cleves, Katherine Howard and Katherine Parr, but he had no more children. Perhaps it was the doubtful right of the Tudors to the throne which had led to Henry's obsession with an heir. As it turned out, all three of Henry's children, Edward, Mary and Elizabeth, succeeded to the throne, one after another, but the Tudor dynasty was to end there, lasting only three generations. None of Henry's children would have children of their own.

The painting shows Henry VIII in the last years of his reign, with his three children and his favourite wife, Jane Seymour. (It was common practice for portraits to include representations of people who had died, alongside the living.) Also in the painting in the background are a male and a female jester, Will and Jane.

Henry VIII in love (2)

Mine own sweetheart, these shall be to advertise you of the great elengeness that I find here since your departing, for I ensure you methinketh the time longer since your departing now last than I was wont to do a whole fortnight . . . Wishing myself (specially an evening) in my sweetheart's arms, whose pretty dukkys I trust shortly to kiss.

(Letter from Henry VIII to Anne Boleyn)

Compare this letter to the poem to Catherine of Aragon on p. 18. What differences do you notice?

Are these differences just because one is a letter and one a poem, or do you think there are other reasons?

Compare this letter to the poem to Catherine of Aragon on p. 18.

CAN YOU REMEMBER ?

the names of Henry VIII's three children, and their mothers?

the names of Henry VIII's other three wives, who did not bear him any children?

The most lasting, though unintentional, change of Henry VIII's reign was religious. Henry VIII's casting off of the authority of the Pope opened the way for the Church of England to become a Protestant church. The basic meaning of *Protestant* is simply someone who makes a protest, and in this case the protest was against the Pope. In sixteenth-century Europe it also came to mean someone who objected to the teaching of the Catholic church, and to its wealth and commercialism (see also page 24–5).

(see also page 24–5).

CHECK YOUR UNDERSTANDING

What do the following words mean?

Annulment
Protestant
Dissolution

THINGS TO DO

1 In groups of three or four, imagine you are the Abbot of Glastonbury and some of his monks, just before Cromwell's investigators arrive. Discuss how you will prepare for their arrival, and what kind of reception you will give them. Are you afraid of them? Who can you trust? How would you cope with being turned out of your monastery, if it came to that?

2 It has been said that the sixteenth century was a very religious age. How sincerely religious do you consider the following to have been: Cardinal Wolsey, Henry VIII, Catherine of Aragon, Anne Boleyn, Thomas Cromwell, Sir Thomas More, the Abbot of Glastonbury? Which of them would you have expected to be most religious?

The dissolution (closure) of the monasteries

Henry's new Archbishop of Canterbury, Thomas Cranmer, and his new chief minister, Thomas Cromwell, who between them successfully achieved the king's divorce, were Protestant in belief. Cromwell was determined to complete the break with Rome by closing the monasteries and nunneries, because their inhabitants still recognized the authority of the Pope. He organized a survey of all the religious houses in England, and discovered that the monks and nuns owned about a quarter of England's fertile land. The survey (called the *Valor Ecclesiasticus*) tried to find evidence to suggest that the monks and nuns were behaving immorally, and breaking their vows to live in poverty.

We came to Glastonbury on Friday last past, about ten of the clock in the forenoon . . . we examined him [the abbot] in certain articles. And for that his answer was not then to our purpose, we advised him to call to his remembrance that which he had then forgotten . . . and then . . . proceeded that night to search his study for letters and books; and found in his study secretly laid a written book of arguments against the divorce of the king's majesty . . . we have found a fair chalice of gold, and . . . other parcels [quantities] of plate, which the abbot had secretly hid . . . and yet he knoweth not we have found the same . . .

(Letter to Thomas Cromwell)

Q

Do you think the Abbot of Glastonbury had really 'forgotten' anything?

How would you describe the methods of the investigators?

Would Thomas Cromwell have found their evidence useful?

Glastonbury is one of the many monasteries that were destroyed during the dissolution of the monasteries.

By 1539 all the monasteries and nunneries were closed. The monks and nuns mostly received pensions from the king, but this did nothing to help the real sufferers, the poor whom the monks and nuns had always looked after (see The Tudor Age, page 8). Meanwhile, Sir Thomas More, who wrote *Utopia* (see p. 10), had been executed for refusing to give his support to the divorce and the break with Rome. The king took over all the monastic lands, buildings and valuables. During the rest of his reign, he sold most of them, and squandered the money on further unsuccessful wars, which achieved nothing.

EDWARD VI – THE BOY KING

Edward VI succeeded to the throne when he was only nine years old. His father had intended that the Council would rule for him, but this never happened. Within three days of Henry VIII's death, Edward's uncle (the brother of his mother Jane Seymour) had taken power as Lord Protector. He bought off the rest of the Council by giving them property and titles, and himself became Duke of Somerset. Somerset was a complex man, ambitious and arrogant, though apparently with some feeling for the sufferings of the poor. His first notable action was to win a remarkable victory against the Scots at the battle of Pinkie Cleugh. It was good publicity for Somerset, but it achieved nothing except to drive the Scots into alliance with the French – hardly a useful move.

The Scottish King James V, whose father had been killed at Flodden when James was a baby, had died in 1542 leaving another infant monarch, Mary Queen of Scots. The Scots arranged a marriage between Mary and the French *Dauphin* (heir to the throne of France).

As well as war, Somerset had to deal with religious and economic problems. Thomas Cranmer was still Archbishop of Canterbury, and both he and Somerset were believers in more Protestant ideas than Henry VIII's. So too, was Edward VI himself, though his beliefs did not really count at this stage as he was too young to have much influence. Protestants thought that the Catholic practice of having paintings and statues in churches encouraged *idolatry* (worshipping images rather than God, a practice forbidden in the Ten Commandments), and distracted the congregation. Cranmer therefore ordered that all paintings and statues should be removed from churches.

In this painting by an unknown artist, you can see the Protestant Edward VI and the defeated Catholic Pope.

In 1549 Cranmer produced a more Protestant prayer book, setting out the order of communion service (the word Mass was no longer used because of its Catholic associations). The service was in English now instead of Latin, because Protestants believed that everyone should be able to understand the proceedings. There was much more participation by the congregation in the new service. The people of Devon and Cornwall were horrified by all this. They thought the service had lost its holiness, and was now just like a 'Christmas game', with everybody taking part. They demanded 'the mass in Latin, as was before' and 'images to be set up again in every church'. They rebelled, and besieged Exeter; the rebellion raged all summer before it was finally put down by Somerset's troops.

At the same time, another rebellion was going on in Norfolk, led by Robert Kett. Enclosures and the price rise (see page 8) were both causing considerable hardship, and Kett collected 16,000 men at Norwich to protest. Their main grievances were high rents and landlords grazing their animals on the common land, which was supposed to be for the use of tenants. This rebellion was particularly serious as Somerset was already preoccupied with the rebellion in the West Country. It had to be dealt with by an army led by John Dudley, the Earl of Warwick.

Even though the rebellions were crushed, people began to lose confidence in Somerset. In contrast, the Earl of Warwick's reputation was greatly enhanced. The Council decided to trust him rather than Somerset, and Somerset was imprisoned in the Tower of London. Warwick did not become Lord Protector, but he dominated the Council for the rest of Edward's reign, and was made Duke of Northumberland in 1551. In 1552 he introduced an even more Protestant prayer book, again written by Cranmer, which was designed to remove the last remnants of anything mystical or superstitious from the communion service. The communion was now just a remembrance service, to commemorate the Last Supper. There was no more question of the bread and wine becoming in a mystical way, as the Catholics believed, the actual body and blood of Jesus (the Protestants scornfully called this magic).

By this time, although the country's economic problems were still worrying, there was no longer any serious opposition to Northumberland. The boy King Edward himself had always been popular anyway, and struck people by his intelligence and courteous behaviour. He seemed to be destined to be a successful king when he became old enough to rule by himself.

But disaster struck in the spring of 1552 in the shape of a bad attack of what was probably measles, which left Edward seriously weakened. By the end of that year he had caught tuberculosis, which until the twentieth century was incurable. It was clear that he would not survive to be an adult. In July 1553 he died.

'A marvellous boy'

Here are two extracts from descriptions of Edward VI:

> an angel in human form; for it was impossible to imagine a more beautiful face and figure, set off by the brilliance of jewels and robes, and a mass of diamonds, rubies and pearls, emeralds and sapphire – they made the whole room look as if lit up.
>
> (Carlois, Secretary to the French Ambassador, quoted in June Osborne, *Hampton Court Palace*)

> nor was he ignorant, as I hear, of the Greek, Italian and Spanish, and perhaps some more. But for the English, French and Latin, he was great in them and apt to learn everything. Nor was he ignorant of logic, of the principles of natural philosophy [science], nor of music . . . These things are not spoken . . . beyond the truth, but are indeed short of it. He was a marvellous boy.
>
> (Giralamo Cardano, quoted in Burnet, *History of the Reformation*)

At the time the first extract was written, there were talks with the French for an alliance between England and France. This was to have been brought about by Edward marrying the French Princess Elisabeth and might explain the splendid impression which the secretary to the French ambassador gave of Edward VI. Or perhaps he just got a bit carried away in his description. What do you think? Pick out the sentence in the second extract which claims that this author is *not* exaggerating.

Q

Do you think Edward might have felt frustrated at having to be King as a teenager?

He also liked jousting and hunting. There is a book called *The Prince and the Pauper*, by Mark Twain (which has also been made into a film), which imagines how Edward liked to change places with a poor boy, in order to enjoy more freedom.

Thomas Cranmer, by Gerlach Flicke.

Cornwall and the new Prayer Book

We will not receive the new service because it is but like a Christmas game, but we will have our old service of Matins, Mass, Evensong and procession in Latin not in English, as it was before. And so we the Cornish men (whereof certain of us understand no English) utterly refuse this new English.

(From the demands of the Western rebels, in *A Copy of a Letter, 1549*)

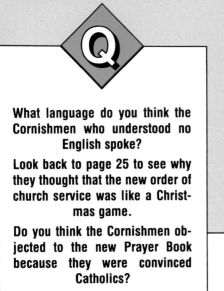

What language do you think the Cornishmen who understood no English spoke?

Look back to page 25 to see why they thought that the new order of church service was like a Christmas game.

Do you think the Cornishmen objected to the new Prayer Book because they were convinced Catholics?

What other reason is suggested by this source?

The painting on page 24, which was probably painted in Elizabeth's reign, shows Edward VI, with the Pope, defeated, at his feet. Somerset sits on his left, and his Council round about, with Cranmer two to the left of that. In bed is the dying King Henry VIII. This is a kind of flashback, in which Henry VIII seems to be blessing Edward VI as his heir. The inset shows Protestants pulling down Catholic images.

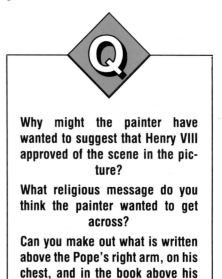

Why might the painter have wanted to suggest that Henry VIII approved of the scene in the picture?

What religious message do you think the painter wanted to get across?

Can you make out what is written above the Pope's right arm, on his chest, and in the book above his head?

CAN YOU REMEMBER ?

the meaning of: Dauphin, idolatry?

which two royal marriages the French planned during Edward's reign?

CHECK YOUR UNDERSTANDING

Was England more Protestant at the end of Edward VI's reign than it had been at the beginning?

THINGS TO DO

1 Imagine you are *either* Edward VI *or* a poor boy who swops places with him. Write an account of your feelings and exeriences during one day of swopping lives.

2 Draw a labelled diagram or cartoon of a Catholic church, showing all the things which Protestants would object to.

On the death of Edward VI, it seemed clear to most people that the next rightful monarch was Henry VIII's elder daughter, Mary. Edward himself, however, aware of his approaching death, had wanted to exclude the Catholic Mary from the throne. He wanted the throne to go to the Lady Jane Grey, who was the Protestant granddaughter of Henry VIII's younger sister. The Duke of Northumberland, who had arranged a marriage between Lady Jane and his own son Guilford Dudley, plotted to bring this about.

But it was Mary who was the popular choice. People rallied to her support, not so much because she was Catholic, as because she was the daughter of Henry VIII. She succeeded to the throne without any serious opposition. The Duke of Northumberland, his son Guilford Dudley and Lady Jane herself were all eventually executed, though at first Mary seemed reluctant to order this fate.

Despite Mary's initial popularity, however, by the end of her reign many of the English were to regret that Mary had ever succeeded to the throne. This was because she threw all her energies into bringing about her dearest wish, to restore England to the Catholic faith. In the sixteenth century, few people ever considered the idea that Catholics could be Catholics and Protestants could be Protestants, without interference. People thought that, if there was only one faith, it was wicked to let others continue in any other faith. They did not understand the contradiction in both sides believing equally that their own particular faith was the only right one.

It was only after encountering opposition that Mary took a really hard line about religion. The opposition was in the form of a rebellion led by Sir Thomas Wyatt against Mary's marriage to her cousin, the Catholic Philip II of Spain. Mary was shaken and hurt by the rebellion. She had been unwilling to marry anyway, preferring to lead a *celibate* (unmarried) life. She realized, however, that she had to marry in order to produce a Catholic heir to the throne. Otherwise it would go to the Protestant Princess Elizabeth. She decided that she would have no one but Philip as her husband. Sir Thomas Wyatt was a Catholic himself, but he hated Spain. His hatred led him to death by execution on Tower Hill.

Wyatt's Rebellion determined Mary to crack down on Protestants. She asked Parliament to re-enact an old Heresy Act of 1401, under which heretics could be burned. (*Heresy* is believing ideas which are not the official ideas of the church. *Heretics* are those who adopt these unofficial ideas.) Parliament agreed, in return for a promise that Mary would not take back from them the monastic lands they had bought from the Crown when

Philip II of Spain, Mary's husband.

Lady Jane Grey. Turn to the family tree on page 30 to see what her claim to the throne was.

Mary I aged 28, painted 3 years before she became queen.

Henry VIII dissolved the monasteries. The most prominent Protestants, including Archbishop Cranmer himself, were burned at the stake. Some of them displayed a courage which seemed to make their martyrdom an inspiration rather than a deterrent to other Protestants. 'Be of good cheer, Master Ridley', cried Father Latimer from the stake at Oxford to his fellow bishop and martyr, 'and play the man. For we shall this day in England light such a fire as shall never be put out.'

Despite all her efforts to re-introduce Catholicism, Mary was unfortunate in not being able to have a baby, the one thing which might have kept England a Catholic country. On two occasions she announced that she was pregnant, but her symptoms turned out not to indicate pregnancy at all. It had never been really likely that she would become pregnant. When she came to the throne at the age of 37, her fertility must already have been declining. Her husband Philip, though kind and concerned, was not often with her, since the affairs of his Spanish kingdom preoccupied him. He was engaged in a European war, a war which England got drawn into as his ally. In this war, the territory around Calais, which was still English (where Henry VIII had met the King of France at the Field of the Cloth of Gold, see page 16), was finally captured by the French.

Mary was to die in 1558, aged 43. Towards the end of her life she fell into a prolonged depression. She said to her lady-in-waiting, 'When I am dead and opened, you will find Calais lying in my heart.' When she died, she was given a Catholic funeral by the new Queen Elizabeth, but after this England was never to be a Catholic country again.

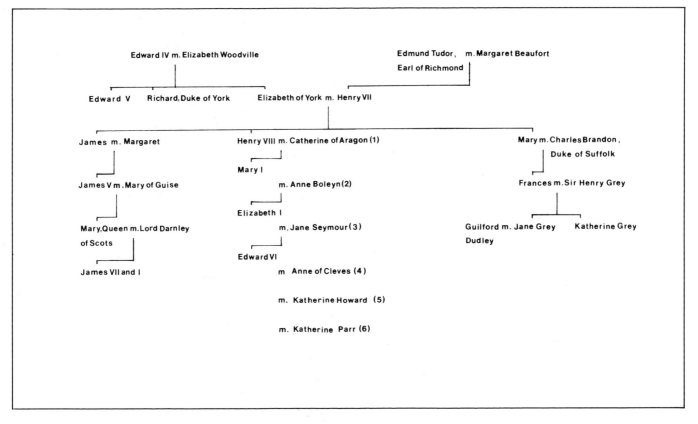

This simplified family tree shows Lady Jane Grey's claim to the throne.

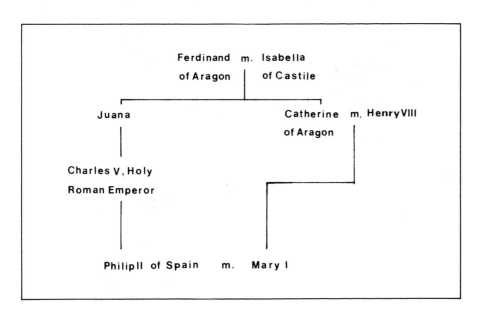

Apart from the children of Henry VIII, is there anyone else who might have claimed the throne?

This family tree shows the relationship between Mary I and her husband, Philip of Spain. It was Philip's father, the Emperor Charles V, who had helped to prevent the Pope from granting Henry's divorce (see Henry VIII – Continuing the Tudor Dynasty, pages 20–23).

You can read more about Father Latimer and Bishop Ridley if you turn back to page 29.

Q

Why do you think they faced their terrible execution so bravely?

Father Latimer and Bishop Ridley were burned at the stake for being Protestants.

CHECK YOUR UNDERSTANDING

What do these words mean?

Heresy
Heretic
Celibate

THINGS TO DO

1 If you could travel back through time, how could you try to dissuade Mary from burning Protestants? Set up a mock television interview or documentary in which both her point of view and an opposing one can be examined.

2 In groups of two or three, draw up a list of topical issues which show that people care just as passionately today about religion as they did in Mary's reign.

CAN YOU WORK OUT ?

why Mary was so hostile to Protestants, and perhaps to Archbishop Cranmer in particular?

CAN YOU REMEMBER ?

what happened to Thomas Cranmer, Archbishop of Canterbury?

The date of Elizabeth I's accession, 17 November, came to be the occasion later in her reign for annual celebration. It was even included in the Church of England's list of Holy Days. In 1558 when she first came to the throne, however, people were not at all sure how they felt about the new queen, or what to expect from her. She was only 25 years old, and it was felt that, like Mary, she would find it difficult both to command respect and to excel in matters of state, because she was a woman. However, she was certainly a daughter of Henry VIII, who was remembered as a strong king and, what is more, she was a Protestant.

She had to be a Protestant for political reasons. Catholics did not recognize the marriage between her mother, Anne Boleyn, and Henry VIII, as they had not recognized the annulment of Henry's first marriage to Catherine of Aragon. Consequently, Catholics regarded Elizabeth as illegitimate, and so not the true heir to the throne. It was therefore necessary for her to change the Church of England back into a Protestant church. In the second year of her reign, Parliament passed an Act of Uniformity, making it illegal to refuse to attend church. Services were to be held using a new Protestant prayer book. Another act was passed which stated that Elizabeth was the Supreme Governor of the Church of England. The English church was Protestant again.

Just as important for Elizabeth at the beginning of her reign was the fact of her gender. It was expected that, like her sister Mary, she would marry. Although prominent men in the state might not welcome a husband of Elizabeth, who might be as unpopular as Mary's husband Philip II of Spain had been, they would welcome the heirs, particularly male ones, which a husband would enable Elizabeth to produce. Elizabeth herself was less convinced that marriage was desirable. She had enough experience of political struggles to be determined to keep power in her own hands. During the course of her long reign she developed a matchless skill at manipulating people and getting her own way.

She did it by making her court into the political arena, so that politics could not be conducted behind her back. She offered honours and financial rewards in return for service, but she granted them only sparingly. So she was able to foster a system in which politicians had to be courtiers, and had to compete with each other in conspicuous devotion to her in order to win her favour. All this attention spoiled her; she was famous for her temper tantrums, and became such a bad loser at cards that she had to be allowed to win. But she successfully held on to her power.

For much of her reign she was also popular among her less powerful subjects, once they too had become used to the idea of a female monarch. 'Oh Lord, the queen is a woman!' exclaimed a London woman, as late as the 1590s. Her popularity was achieved through the efficiency of her propaganda machine, the church. From the pulpit and in their prayers, people were constantly informed how lucky they were in their queen, how much they loved her, and how successfully she was ruling them. They were encouraged to sing ballads about Elizabeth, to wear her portrait and to strain for glimpses of her as she travelled on her royal 'progresses', which were journeys she made with her court to show herself to her people. She stayed (free of charge) with the local nobility, and rarely went out of the Home Counties, but she played her royal role for all it was worth, for maximum publicity. She certainly knew a thing or two about what the modern age might call image-making and marketing.

Towards the end of her reign, it was becoming obvious that Elizabeth's image was very different from the reality. The myth of the youthful and glorious queen was beginning to wear thin; observers noticed her blackened teeth, her rather loud red wig, lead-whitened face and wrinkled neck. Courtier/politicians began to speculate on what their prospects would be like under her successor. But Elizabeth never let go of either her image or her control. It seems symbolic, perhaps, that even when she was dying, she refused to lie down, preferring to die in her chair.

This painting by George Gower is known as the 'Armada' portrait. You can see the Spanish fleet (the Armada) in the background, coming to invade England.

Elizabeth and marriage

It is impossible to say whether Elizabeth would have liked to marry if she had not been queen. She did have a favourite in Robert Dudley, the Earl of Leicester, the youngest son of the Duke of Northumberland. It was Dudley's brother who had been married to Lady Jane Grey (see page 28). A courtier and historian, William Camden, explained his view of Elizabeth's feelings on the matter:

> she was fully resolved in her mind that she might better provide both for the commonwealth [the country] and her own glory by an unmarried life than by marriage . . . if she married a subject she would disparage [lower] herself by the inequality of the match, and give occasion of domestical heartburnings, private grudges and other commotions; if a stranger [foreigner], she would then subject both herself and her people to a foreign yoke, and endanger religion.
>
> (William Camden, *The History of the Most Renowned and Victorious Princess Elizabeth*, 1575)

Eventually, many people came to admire her for her independence, although she did not alter people's opinions of the capabilities of women in general. This is a verse of a ballad written at her death:

> She ruled this nation by herself
> And was beholden to no man
> Oh, she bore the sway of all affairs
> And yet she was but a woman
>
> (Quoted in Christopher Haigh, *Elizabeth I*)

What kind of 'domestical heart-burnings' do you think there might be if Elizabeth married a subject?

Why might religion be endangered if she married a foreigner?

Elizabeth I in 1598

> Next came the Queen, in the sixty-fifth year of her age, as we were told, very majestic; her face oblong, fair, but wrinkled; her eyes small, yet black and pleasant; her nose a little hooked; her lips narrow, and her teeth black (a defect the English seem subject to, for their too great use of sugar); she had in her ears two pearls, with very rich drop; she wore false hair, and that red; upon her head she had a small crown . . . Her bosom was uncovered . . . and she had on a necklace of exceeding fine jewels;
>
> (Paul Hentzner, *A Journey into England in the year 1598*)

How does this description of Elizabeth compare with her portraits on pages 33, 35, 37 and 41?

This picture shows Elizabeth's court on progress around London.

Elizabeth was always careful to do her homework before she visited an area, so that she could flatter the inhabitants by her local knowledge. She could cry at will, and often did so as she left a town, for effect. She put on a particular show leaving Norwich in 1578, telling the mayor she would never forget his town, and bursting into tears crying, 'Farewell, Norwich!' as she left.

CAN YOU REMEMBER ?

who was Elizabeth's mother?

how old Elizabeth was when she came to the throne?

what title Elizabeth took in the Church of England?

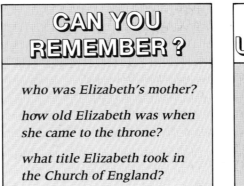

CHECK YOUR UNDERSTANDING

Our characters are often shaped by our experiences. Suggest some possible explanations for why Elizabeth became the kind of person she did.

For many years, historians thought that there were important developments in the power and status of Parliament during the reign of Elizabeth I. The House of Commons, which was traditionally then the least powerful of the two Houses, was thought to have increased its influence. Recent research suggests that this was not really the case. Elizabeth disliked parliament, and summoned only 13 parliaments in her 45 years on the throne. In the previous 30 years, Henry VIII, Edward VI and Mary had summoned between them 28. One of the reasons for her dislike was that the House of Commons could provide an opportunity for discussions of sensitive topics which Elizabeth would have preferred to be glossed over, the question of her marrying, for instance, and the question of religion.

There were certainly some Members of Parliament who were prepared to push as far as they could go in the discussion of these awkward subjects, and to defy the queen when she tried to prevent them being debated. There were people both inside and outside the House of Commons who thought that Elizabeth's religious settlement had left the church 'only half reformed', and in need of further purification from the remnants of Catholicism. People who thought like this were called Puritans. There was a group of them sitting in the House of Commons during much of Elizabeth's reign. They introduced bills for making the Church of England more Protestant, and attacked Catholicism at every opportunity. Two brothers from Cornwall, Peter and Paul Wentworth, complained loudly about the queen's attempts to stop them discussing religion, and claimed she was violating the Commons' privilege of free speech. They did not have a large following in the House of Commons, though. Their attacks on the queen received great publicity, but it was out of proportion to their importance.

For it was only a small number of individuals who were prepared to go anything like as far as the Wentworths. Behind those that were was often one or other of the queen's councillors, who having failed to make any headway against Elizabeth's stubbornness in council, hoped to get further with a more public airing of their point of view. Some of the Council were definitely inclined

towards Puritanism. All of them were anti-Catholic, and very wary about the possibility that she might be succeeded on the throne by Mary Queen of Scots, her Catholic cousin. This possibility came closer once it became clear that Elizabeth was unlikely to have her own child. For the 15 years between 1572 and 1587, the Council, led by Elizabeth's secretary, William Cecil, waged a campaign to try to persuade Elizabeth to agree to exclude Mary Queen of Scots from the succession to the throne. They used parliamentary debate to try to put pressure on her.

Eventually, the Council had its way. Mary had been a focus for Catholic discontent, a centre of Catholic plots since she had been driven from the throne of Scotland by Scottish Protestants in 1568 and taken refuge in England. Finally in 1587, she was shown to have taken part in a conspiracy to overthrow Elizabeth, though she may well have been framed by Sir Francis Walsingham, one of Elizabeth's Puritan councillors. Whatever the truth behind this, Elizabeth now felt she had no choice but to excute Mary.

It is hard to know how effective parliamentary pressure had been in forcing Elizabeth's hand. Elizabeth's parliaments were always more anti-Catholic than she was, more anti-Spanish in foreign policy, and much more concerned about the succession. Elizabeth's main concern was not to plan for the future, but to keep things as they were, and to fend off threats to her position. In a real crisis, such as the threatened invasion by the Spanish Armada in 1588, she was magnificent, rallying her troops at Tilbury with her presence and inspiring words. Behind the scenes in day to day politics she could be childish, small minded and incapable of making decisions.

Bad harvests and economic problems beset the last years of her reign, and by the time she died the 'Gloriana' myth of virtue and splendour, which she had worked so hard to create, had worn very thin. After her death, though, it revived. Perhaps she was not the 'Good Queen Bess' she might have liked to be thought, but in some ways her reign was successful. She established a church which, although it pleased neither Catholics nor Puritans, still forms the basis of the Church of England today. She forged a successful partnership with the

Mary Queen of Scots.

Here, Elizabeth I is rallying the troops at Tilbury, urging them on in the face of the Spanish Armada.

gentry who, as *Justices of the Peace*, administered local government and law and order in the localities. She kept the country out of major wars. She coped adequately if not spectacularly with the social and economic pressures of inflation. What is more, she set a *precedent* (first-time example) for successful female rule, so that the sex of an heir was never again such an issue as it had been under Henry VIII.

Trouble in Parliament

It was always in the House of Commons that any trouble arose, never the House of Lords, where the noblemen and bishops who sat there remained totally loyal to Elizabeth. This is an extract from Peter Wentworth's speech made in 1576. Peter Wentworth is addressing the Speaker (chairman) as all MPs must, when they speak in the House of Commons.

> Certain it is, Mr Speaker, that none is without fault, no, not our noble Queen, since her Majesty hath committed great fault, yea dangerous faults to herself.

This is what happened next day in the House of Commons:

> touching the violent and wicked words yesterday pronounced by him in this house touching the Queen's majesty . . . which words . . . the said Peter Wentworth did acknowledge and confess . . . . It was ordered . . . that the said Peter Wentworth should be committed close prisoner to the Tower for his said offence.

> (Sir Simonds D'Ewes, *Journals of the Parliaments of the Reign of Queen Elizabeth I*)

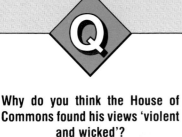

Why do you think the House of Commons found his views 'violent and wicked'?

Did Peter Wentworth try to wriggle out of trouble?

Nothing dreadful happened to him in the Tower of London, and he was still causing trouble well into the 1590s!

This sketch shows simultaneously three stages in the execution of Mary Queen of Scots. On the left, you can see her coming in through the door; in the centre, she is being prepared; and at the back of the central enclosure, she is being executed.

Mary Queen of Scots

Mary, Mary, quite contrary,
How does your garden grow?
With silver bells, and cockle shells
And pretty maids all in a row.

Some people say this nursery rhyme refers to Mary Queen of Scots. In this case, the silver bells might be the bells rung during the Mass. The cockle shells could be the badges of Catholic pilgrims to the shrine of St James in Spain, or even the embroidered motifs on a dress she had been given by the Dauphin, her childhood husband (see page 24). The pretty maids might be her attendants, her famous four Marys, Mary Beaton, Mary Seton, Mary Carmichael and Mary Hamilton. Have you any idea why Mary herself might be called contrary?

Elizabeth and Mary never met, although they were cousins. Elizabeth was jealous of Mary's famed beauty, but always regarded her as a fellow monarch, and was very reluctant to bring Mary to trial and to sign her death warrant when she was found guilty. This was an occasion when Elizabeth may have been outmanoeuvred by her more Puritan councillors, who wanted Mary out of the way (see page 36). Despite her execution, it was Mary's descendants who were the future rulers of England, as you can see from the family tree. Elizabeth had no heirs at all.

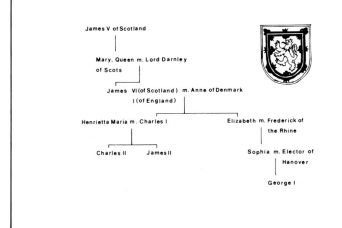

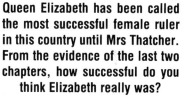

Queen Elizabeth has been called the most successful female ruler in this country until Mrs Thatcher. From the evidence of the last two chapters, how successful do you think Elizabeth really was?

CHECK YOUR UNDERSTANDING

What do these words mean?

Puritan
Precedent
Speaker

CAN YOU REMEMBER ?

the names of the troublesome MPs?

who the nursery rhyme 'Mary, Mary' is said to be based on, and what it might mean?

THINGS TO DO

Find out more about the Spanish Armada. There were large numbers of books and pamphlets produced about it in 1988, on the 400th anniversary of its defeat.

The Tudors established a new image of monarchy. In the century before Henry VII came to the throne, it was not unusual for kings to be *deposed* (forced from the throne). Kings found it hard to establish their authority over powerful nobles, from whose ranks they had very often come themselves. But the Tudors, even though their dynasty only lasted three generations, succeeded in convincing the country that their rule was both legitimate and permanent. When Elizabeth was succeeded by James I, James's descent from Henry VII (plus his Protestantism) ensured his unopposed succession.

Tudor monarchy was established in various ways. Of course, it helped that Henry VII had taken such a tough line with the nobles who might have challenged him (see page 12). Both his granddaughters, Mary and Elizabeth, had similar views on preventing aristocratic challenge. Elizabeth never raised anyone to the position of duke, and England was left with no dukes at all after 1572 when the Duke of Norfolk was executed for his part in a Catholic rebellion.

Creating an image of powerful monarchy was also important. Tudor monarchs readily resorted to what we today call propaganda, both written and pictorial. The invention of the printing press helped. William Caxton's first press in London had already printed its first book ten years before the beginning of Henry VII's reign. Printing helped to stimulate the writing of history, which could be useful propaganda for Tudor rule. Polydore Vergil, an Italian, was encouraged by Henry VII to write a history (see page 15) in which, while sometimes criticizing aspects of royal government, he emphasized that Henry VII was right to seize the throne from Richard III, because Richard III, he says, ruled unjustly.

A History of Richard III, written by Sir Thomas More (see page 42) in Henry VIII's reign, also claims that Richard III had been evil and unjust. Both books served to remind people that Tudor stability compared very favourably with the civil wars of the years before 1485.

Another influential publication was an English translation of the stories of King Arthur and the Round Table, which Caxton printed in 1484.

Henry VII made a point of identifying himself with King Arthur and other former British kings, and named his eldest son Arthur (see page 16). This, too, was part of the bid to create an image of the king as legitimate, powerful and unassailable.

Henry VII was lucky too that the Pope gave his blessing to his marriage to Elizabeth of York. When another Pope was later defied by Henry VIII (see page 20), even this boosted royal status, because Henry VIII became Supreme Head of the English church. The English liked the idea that their king and country could not be controlled from abroad.

Later in the sixteenth century, another writer whose works supported the monarchy was William Shakespeare. 'Is not the King's name twenty thousand names?' asks Richard II, in Shakespeare's play.

It was a fortunate coincidence that the Tudors also lived at a time of great achievement in the art of portraiture. The portraits of Henry VIII by Hans Holbein conveyed power, majesty and just a hint of threat. Portraits of Elizabeth are familiar for their characteristic emphasis on her dresses and jewels (see page 33). Though many artists were involved in producing them, they were painted to quite a small number of patterns, which had to be officially approved. English painters were particularly skilled at painting miniatures, sometimes only a few inches in area, with brushes composed of only one or two hairs. The older Elizabeth grew, the more timeless and ageless the patterns became. The famous 'Ditchley' portrait became the official *template* (pattern) for the 1590s.

Together with the ballads, sonnets and poems written and sung about Elizabeth, her visual image became central to propaganda in her reign (see also pages 32–5). By the end of the century, the idea of the Queen as an object of reverence, admiration, love and respect was consolidated. The cult of Queen Elizabeth was like a very well-organized fan club.

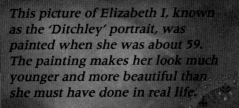

After more then 100 years of Tudor rule, the idea that the Tudors were monarchs purely because Henry VII had been lucky enough to defeat Richard III in battle was unthinkable. The Tudors had established, even invented, the idea of monarchy as glorious and blessed by God. They may not always have been totally successful at governing the country, but as image makers they were unbeatable.

Polydore Vergil and Sir Thomas More on Richard III

He reigned two years, one month, and twenty-seven days. He was but of a small stature, having but a deformed body, the one shoulder was higher than the other; . . . and while he did muse upon anything . . . he would bite his underlip continually, whereby a man might perceive his cruel nature.

(Sir Thomas More, *History of Richard III*, 1510–18)

He reigned two years and so many months and one day over. He was little of stature, deformed of body, the one shoulder being higher than the other . . . The while he was thinking of any matter, he did continually bite his nether lip, as though that cruel nature of his did rage against itself in that little carcase.

(Polydore Vergil, *English History*, 1512–13)

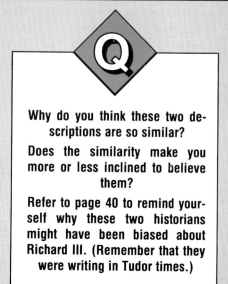

Why do you think these two descriptions are so similar?

Does the similarity make you more or less inclined to believe them?

Refer to page 40 to remind yourself why these two historians might have been biased about Richard III. (Remember that they were writing in Tudor times.)

Shakespeare on monarchy

Shakespeare suggests that nothing can stop a king being a king, once he has been *anointed* (touched with sacred *balm*, or oil, at his coronation):

> Nor all the water in the rough, rude sea,
> Can wash the balm off from an anointed king.

(*Richard II*)

The following lines, which refer to Elizabeth, must have kept Shakespeare in favour with the queen:

> She shall be loved and feared: her own shall bless her;
> Her foes shake like a field of beaten corn,
> And hang their heads with sorrow: good grows with her.
> In her days every man shall eat in safety,
> Under his own vine, what he plants; and sing
> The merry songs of peace to all his neighbours.

(*Henry VIII*)

Elizabethan propaganda verses

The rose is red, the leaves are green,
God save Elizabeth, our noble queen.

(Written by a schoolboy on his Latin reader, 1589)

Earth is now green, and heaven is blue,
Lively spring which makes all new,
Iolly spring doth enter,
Sweet young sunbeams do subdue
Angry, aged winter.

(John Davies, *Hymns to Astraea*)

What tells you that the last verse is about Elizabeth? (Look at the first letter of each line. Now you'll see why Jolly is written Iolly!) Elizabeth is being compared to Spring, even though this poem was written in 1599 when she was 66 years old.

Can you imagine doodling a poem about *our* queen on one of your school textbooks?

Who would you be more likely to doodle about?

THINGS TO DO

1 Today's propaganda methods are the same as those used by commercial advertising. Plan a television commercial or a promotional video advertising one of the Tudor monarchs.

2 Make a 'Tudor Monarchs' collage, either with or without written comments, showing what you think is important about their reigns.

3 In groups of two or three, discuss the advantages and disadvantages of the kind of monarchy practised by the Tudors, where the monarch had a great deal of personal power.

4 Look back through this book and make a list of all the paintings that seem to have a propaganda purpose. How do they try to influence the person looking at them?

CAN YOU REMEMBER ?

the meaning of propaganda, legitimate, depose, template, anoint, balm? (Propaganda and legitimate are words used in previous chapters.)

CHECK YOUR UNDERSTANDING

Do you think the images we see of politicians and the royal family in the media today have a propaganda purpose?

One way of spreading propaganda about the Tudor monarchs was through plays. This engraving shows a play by William Shakespeare being performed.

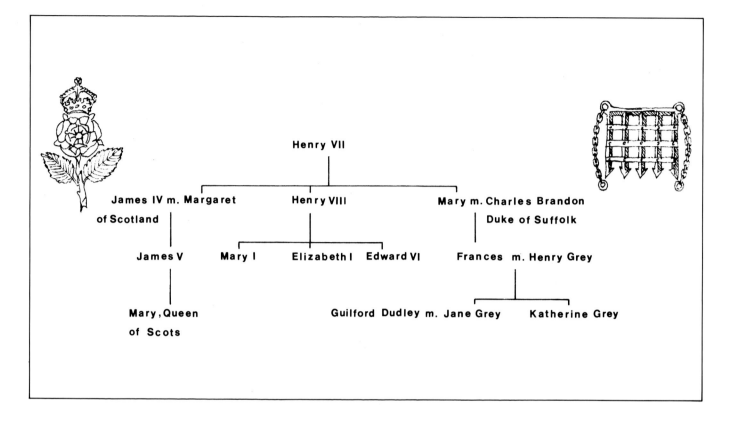

TIME CHART

1485	End of Wars of the Roses
	Henry VII becomes king
1501	Death of Prince Arthur
1509	Henry VIII becomes king
1513	Battle of Flodden
1515	Wolsey becomes Chancellor
1516	Birth of Mary
1520	Field of the Cloth of Gold
1533	Henry marries Anne Boleyn
	Birth of Elizabeth
1536	Anne Boleyn executed
	Henry marries Jane Seymour
1537	Birth of Edward
	Jane Seymour dies
1536–39	Dissolution of the monasteries
1547	Edward VI becomes king (Somerset is Protector)
1549	Edward VI's First Protestant prayer book
	Western Rebellion
	Kett's Rebellion
1551	Northumberland seizes power
1552	Edward VI's Second Protestant prayer book
1553	Mary becomes queen
	Execution of Lady Jane Grey, Northumberland and Guilford Dudley
1554	Wyatt's Rebellion
1558	Elizabeth becomes queen
1568	Mary Queen of Scots flees to England
1587	Execution of Mary Queen of Scots
1588	Defeat of the Spanish Armada
1603	Death of Elizabeth
	The end of the Tudor Age

GLOSSARY

annulment   declaration that something is invalid

anoint   to touch with holy oil

balm   holy or healing oil or juice

cardinal   holder of the highest rank (under the Pope) in the Catholic church

celibate   unmarried

consummate   to complete a marriage by sexual union

Dauphin   the heir to the French throne

depopulation   driving tenants off the land in order to use the land for raising sheep (*see* **enclosure**)

depose   force from the throne

dissolution (of monasteries)   closing down

dynasty   family of rulers in which power is passed down from parent to child

enclosure   agricultural change from growing crops to raising sheep, which involved fencing off fields

feudal   a relationship between different ranks of society, in which the rich and powerful gave land to others in return for work and military service

Gloriana   the nickname given to Elizabeth I, suggesting she was the embodiment of virtue, splendour and glory

heresy   belief in ideas which are not the official ideas of the church

heretic   someone whose ideas are heresy (*see above*)

idolatry   worshipping images instead of God

inflation   rising prices

intelligence service   means of gathering information through spies and informers

Justice of the Peace   local, unpaid official who is responsible for maintaining law and order

legitimate   (i) lawful
(ii) being the true child of legally married parents, and thus your father's legal heir

martyr   someone who dies for their beliefs

ostler   someone who looks after horses, usually at an inn

Papal Legate   representative of the Pope outside Rome

portcullis   gate to a fort or castle, made of crossed iron or wooden struts

precedent   something which having been done once serves as an example in similar cases

propaganda   political advertising, or spreading of a particular point of view for political purposes

Protestant   someone who refused to accept the authority of the Pope

Puritan   someone who wanted to get rid of all the remains of Catholic ideas from the Church of England

shrine   holy place, usually dedicated to a saint

Speaker   the chairman of the House of Commons

template   pattern

vagrant   someone who is homeless, and therefore wanders about begging or stealing

Valor Ecclesiasticus   literally, the strength of the church – this was a survey of the monasteries and nunneries organized by Thomas Cromwell

virginals   early keyboard instrument

Do you know?

The names, in order, of all the Tudor monarchs?

Why it was important to Henry VII that he should marry Elizabeth of York?

Who built Hampton Court, and why it passed into the ownership of the crown?

Why Henry VIII closed the monasteries?

Who wrote the first English Prayer Books?

Why Mary I is sometimes known as 'Bloody Mary'?

Why Mary Queen of Scots is important in English history as well as Scottish?

What the Spanish Armada was?

Whether each of the Tudor monarchs was Catholic or Protestant?

What propaganda means?

FURTHER READING

June Osborne, *Entertaining Elizabeth I*, Bishopsgate, 1989

(ed) Jasper Ridley, *The Love Letters of Henry VIII*, Cassell, 1988

Neville Williamson, *Henry VIII*, Weidenfeld and Nicolson, 1973

Jasper Ridley, *Mary Tudor*, Weidenfeld and Nicolson, 1973

Stephen White-Thomson, *Elizabeth I and Tudor England*, Wayland, 1984

S.M. Harrison, *Elizabeth in Danger*, Macmillan, 1984

Geoffrey Regan, *Elizabethan England*, Batsford, 1990

David McDowall, *The Spanish Armada*, Batsford, 1988

Michael Palmer, *Elizabeth I*, Batsford, 1988

David Anderson, *The Spanish Armada*, MacDonald, 1988

INDEX